Published in 2014 by The Rosen Publishing Group, Inc.
29 East 21st Street, New York, NY 10010

Photo Credits: **KEY** tl=top left; tc=top center; tr=top right; cl=center left; cr=center right; bl=bottom left; right; br=bottom right

CBT = Corbis; GI = Getty Images; iS = istockphoto.com; SH = Shutterstock; SPL = Science Photo Library; TF = Topfoto; TPL = photolibrary.com

8tr CBT; tl, tr iS; **9**tl, tr, bl, br CBT; **11**br CBT; **16**bl GI; **17**tr CBT; **18**cl, cr, tc TF; **19**c CBT; cr, tc, tl TF; **20**cl, cr, tl CBT; **21**c, tl CBT; **23**c CBT; **24**bc iS; tr SH; cl TPL; **24–25**bc iS; **25**cr, tl CBT; tr iS; br TPL; **29**c, tl SPL; **30**tr CBT; cr iS

All illustrations copyright Weldon Owen Pty Ltd

Weldon Owen Pty Ltd
Managing Director: Kay Scarlett
Creative Director: Sue Burk
Publisher: Helen Bateman
Senior Vice President, International Sales: Stuart Laurence
Vice President Sales North America: Ellen Towell
Administration Manager, International Sales: Kristine Ravn

Library of Congress Cataloging-in-Publication Data

Coupe, Robert.
 Dinosaur hunters / by Robert Coupe.
   pages cm. — (Discovery education : discoveries and inventions)
 Includes index.
 ISBN 978-1-4777-1328-0 (library binding) — ISBN 978-1-4777-1498-0 (pbk.) —
ISBN 978-1-4777-1499-7 (6-pack)
 1. Dinosaurs—Juvenile literature. 2. Paleontologists—Juvenile literature. I. Title.
 QE861.5.C68 2014
 567.9—dc23
                                     2012043618

Manufactured in the United States of America

CPSIA Compliance Information #S13PK3: For Further Information contact Rosen Publishing, New York, New York at 1-800-237-9932

Discovery CORPORATION

DISCOVERIES AND INVENTIONS

DINOSAUR HUNTERS

ROBERT COUPE

PowerKiDS press

New York

Contents

Finding Fossils

The last true dinosaurs that lived on Earth died out about 65 million years ago. Some dinosaur bones remain preserved and buried in the ground or in rocky cliffs in many parts of the world. These preserved bones are called fossils. The people who search for, find, and study these fossils are paleontologists. Sometimes, they find tiny fragments of preserved bones. Other times, they find almost whole dinosaur skeletons.

Taking care
While uncovering the bones of a large dinosaur, paleontologists must dig or chip away dirt or rock around the fossil, taking care not to break or damage the bones.

Desert areas
Paleontologists find the preserved bones of many dinosaurs in harsh desert areas. Here, hot dry winds often wear away rocky cliffs and sandy soils, so fossils buried below come closer to the surface. As more dinosaur fossils are found, paleontologists get to know the kinds of places where they are likely to find more dinosaur fossils.

Digging
As diggers uncover more of the dinosaur's skeleton, they begin to dig a trench around and underneath it. This way, they may be able to lift it carefully and in one piece out of the ground.

Notes and maps
Before any bones are removed, paleontologists draw maps of where the skeleton was found. They also make detailed notes about smaller pieces of bones the diggers have discovered.

1. Searching on a dig
Paleontologists search for dinosaur fossils among ancient rocks that have worn away over millions of years. Even tiny pieces of bone can provide important information.

2. Finding a large fossil
Barnum Brown was a famous paleontologist who discovered the remains of many dinosaurs. In August 1934, he found this large dinosaur fossil in Wyoming.

In a Museum

Dinosaur skeletons are often displayed in museums of natural history. Scientists and other technicians carry out important work before the fossils are ready to be displayed in the museum.

Final touches
The bones of the skeleton are connected and held together by metal frames and wires. A technician is responsible for welding these pieces of metal together.

3. Protecting with plaster
Before large fossils can be removed from where they have been found, they are carefully wrapped in foil, plaster, and burlap to protect them from being damaged.

4. Cleaning up
The fossils are unwrapped in a laboratory. Technicians use brushes, saws, chisels, and special machines to remove any pieces of rock and soil that are stuck to the bones.

5. Sorting out
A team of paleontologists lays out the ribs and backbone of a *Tyrannosaurus rex*. The next step will be joining the fossils together to form a complete skeleton.

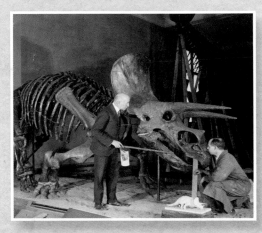

6. Ready for display
Triceratops had long horns and a bony frill behind its head. When its skeleton is displayed in a museum, it is easy to imagine what it looked like when it lived millions of years ago.

Fossil History

Two species of dinosaur, Velociraptor and Protoceratops, lived about 70 million years ago in the country that is now called Mongolia. Velociraptor was a fierce hunter and Protoceratops was a plant-eating dinosaur. One day, a Velociraptor attacked a Protoceratops in a sandy desert. As the two dinosaurs fought, a huge bank of sand collapsed on top of them. They were buried and died, locked together.

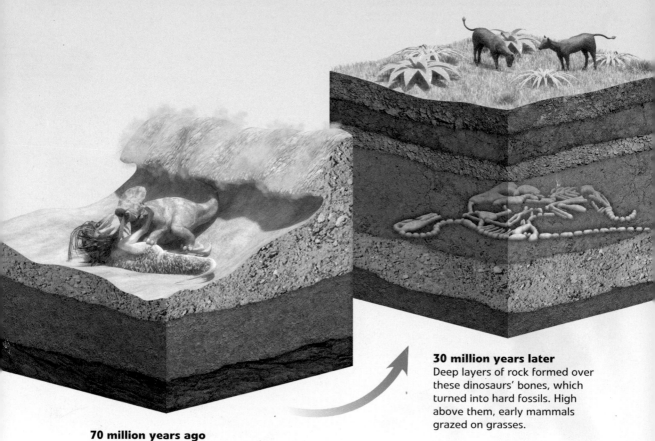

30 million years later
Deep layers of rock formed over these dinosaurs' bones, which turned into hard fossils. High above them, early mammals grazed on grasses.

70 million years ago
Buried deep down under many layers of sand, the dinosaurs' bodies slowly rotted away, but their skeletons, still locked together, did not.

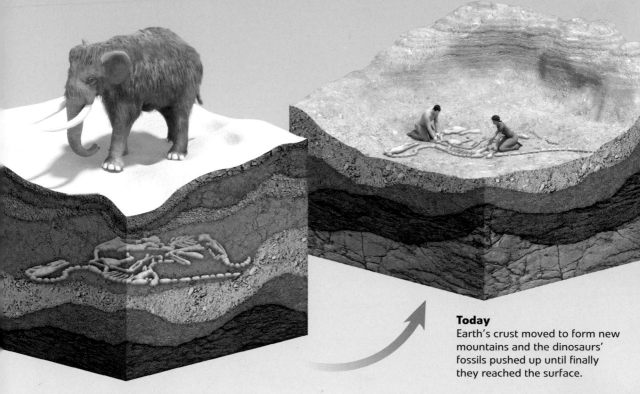

Today
Earth's crust moved to form new mountains and the dinosaurs' fossils pushed up until finally they reached the surface.

20 million years later
During an ice age, huge mammoths lived on Earth. Down below, Earth's crust moved and pushed the fossils upward, closer to the surface.

A true account?

Although this story is probably true, there is a small chance it is not. It is possible that the two dinosaurs died separately in different places. A flood could have washed the two skeletons together and then covered them with sand. Perhaps they only looked as though they were fighting.

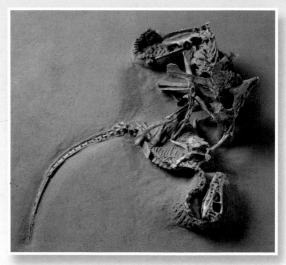

Discovered
Searchers found the exposed dinosaur skeletons, just as they were when they died. Velociraptor's sharp claw is deep inside Protoceratops' ribs.

All About Leonardo

I n July 2000, a fossil hunter in Montana came upon the fossilized body of a dinosaur. The following summer, experts carefully removed the dinosaur, which they called Leonardo, from the rock that surrounded it. When they studied it, they were surprised at what they found.

Looking inside
Not only had Leonardo's bones become fossils, so had some of his skin, muscles, and other soft body parts.

Muscle mass
Fossils of muscle were found attached to Leonardo's bones. These provided clues to how the limbs worked.

Skeleton
Leonardo's skeleton provided clues about his shape and size. It also showed that the dinosaur moved on four legs.

Frill
A frill of thin plates stood up all along Leonardo's back. These were bones that were covered with flesh.

Shoulder muscles
The rock around Leonardo contained imprints of shoulder muscles. These showed how big the muscles were.

Crop
A pouch, or crop, in his throat allowed Leonardo to store and chew large amounts of plant food.

Tongue
The shape of Leonardo's tongue was also preserved in the rock.

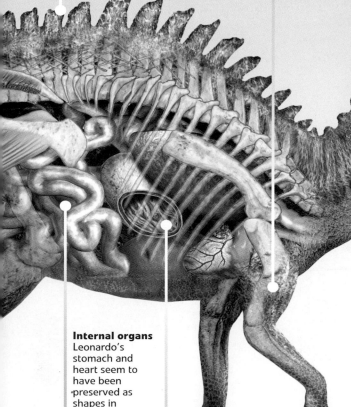

Internal organs
Leonardo's stomach and heart seem to have been preserved as shapes in the rock.

Last meal
Fossils of ferns and other plants were found inside Leonardo's stomach. This confirms he was a plant eater.

LOOKING INSIDE

By using X-rays and scanners to study fossils, scientists can find out about how dinosaurs' bodies worked.

Moving joints
Cartilage between bones allowed bones to move without scraping against each other.

Grooves
Grooves in dinosaur bones show the places where muscles were attached to them.

Muscles
This is how the muscles covering a dinosaur's bone would have looked.

Reading Footprints

Fossils of dinosaur footprints are called trackways. They tell us a lot about how different kinds of dinosaurs lived and moved. For example, trackways indicate that some plant-eating dinosaurs lived and traveled around in large herds. They also show how meat-eating dinosaurs, looking for a meal, followed and caught up with these herds. Trackways also provide clues to how quickly or slowly different dinosaurs could travel.

DIFFERENT TRACKS

Different types of dinosaurs left behind footprints of different shapes and sizes. These help scientists to identify them.

Large meat eaters
These dinosaurs walked on their two back feet. Each back foot had three toes with claws.

A large plant-eating dinosaur could provide a smaller meat eater with enough food for a week.

Chaser
A quick-moving small dinosaur prepares to attack much larger plant-eating dinosaurs.

Safety in numbers

It was safer for plant-eating dinosaurs to move around in large herds. That way, individual dinosaurs had less chance of being caught and eaten. Young dinosaurs traveled in the middle of the herd.

Large plant eaters
Big plant eaters walked around on four feet. Their back feet made bigger prints than their front feet.

Small meat eaters
The trackways left by small meat-eating dinosaurs look very similar to the footprints of today's birds.

Horned dinosaurs
Dinosaurs with horns walked on all fours. Their back feet were larger and had four toes.

Long neck
Many plant eaters had a long neck so they could reach high up into trees.

Other Clues

Different kinds of fossils provide plenty of other information about dinosaurs' lives. Much can be learned from fossils of dinosaur bones and footprints, but other fossils provide clues to what they ate, what their nests were like, and even what kinds of sounds some of them made.

Struthiomimus
This fast-running dinosaur had no teeth. Its mouth was like a bird's beak.

Hooting
Parasaurolophus could send air up into its crest and make loud hooting sounds.

Stomach stones
Struthiomimus had stones in its stomach that helped to grind up plants and seeds.

Parasaurolophus
This dinosaur had a large, hollow crest that stood up high above its head.

Pieces of dung
Fossils of dinosaur dung can show what kind of food was eaten.

Nesting

Many female dinosaurs laid eggs and made nests, just as reptiles and birds do now.

Nest and egg fossils

In 1978, Dr. John Horner found a fossil dinosaur nest in Montana. In it were fossil egg-shells and the fossils of baby dinosaurs.

That's Amazing!

It was not until 1922 that the first fossil dinosaur eggs were discovered. They were found in Mongolia and belonged to a dinosaur that we now call Oviraptor.

EGG SHAPES AND SIZES

Compare the size and shape of different dinosaurs' eggs with a modern hen's egg. Sauropods were large plant eaters with very long necks.

Hen's egg

Protoceratops
Long and thin with bumpy shell

Velociraptor
Long and thin with pointy end

Hypselosaurus
Oval-shaped, football-sized egg

Sauropod
Oval-shaped with rough, bumpy shell

Dinosaur Discoveries

I n addition to Barnum Brown and John Horner, there have been many other famous discoverers of dinosaurs. The next four pages show a time line of the people who ventured into remote and wild places, and the dinosaur remains they found.

Massospondylus

Apatosaurus

Iguanodon

1825
Gideon Mantell (1790–1852) was an English country doctor. In 1822, in southern England, he found the first-ever remains of a dinosaur he named Iguanodon. It means "iguana tooth."

1853
Richard Owen (1804–1892) was an English paleontologist who invented the word "dinosaur," which means "terrible lizard." In 1853, remains of Massospondylus were found in South Africa. Owen gave it its name, which means "massive backbone."

1879
Othniel Charles Marsh (1831–1899) was an American scientist who found and named many dinosaurs. One was Apatosaurus, which means "deceptive dinosaur." Marsh thought some of its bones looked like those of other lizards.

Ornitholestes

Tyrannosaurus rex

Protoceratops

1880s
Edward Drinker Cope (1840–1897) and Othniel Marsh were rivals, each trying to discover more dinosaurs than the other. Between them they found hundreds of dinosaur fossils in North America.

1902
In 1902, Barnum Brown (1873–1963) discovered, in Montana fossil remains of the most famous dinosaur of all—the ferocious hunter *Tyrannosaurus rex*.

1903
Henry Fairfield Osborn (1857–1935) was an American paleontologist. In 1903, he described and named the dinosaur Ornitholestes, meaning "bird robber."

1923
Roy Chapman Andrews (1884–1960), an American, led expeditions to Mongolia during the 1920s. One of several dinosaurs discovered on these expeditions, in 1923, was Protoceratops.

Maiasaura

Deinonychus

Carnotaurus

1964
John Ostrom (1928–2005) discovered Deinonychus in Montana in 1964. This small meat eater had a sharp claw, shaped like a sickle, on each foot. The name Ostrom chose means "terrible claw."

1978
John "Jack" Horner (born 1946) is an American paleontologist. His most famous discovery was in 1978 in Montana where he found fossil nests and eggs of a new species of dinosaur. Horner named this dinosaur Maiasaura, which means "good mother lizard."

1980–2000s
Professor Dong Zhiming (born 1937) has probably discovered and named more dinosaurs than any other scientist. He has found most of these in northern China and Mongolia.

1985
José Bonaparte (born 1928) lives in Argentina and has discovered and named many South American dinosaurs. One, in 1985, was an almost complete skeleton of Carnotaurus, meaning "meat bull."

Caudipteurix

Herrerasaurus

1986
Robert Bakker (born 1945) wrote *The Dinosaur Heresies* in 1986, as well as many other books that describe how dinosaurs lived and what they were like. We now understand that many of them were very active and agile animals.

1988
American Paul Sereno (born 1957) and Argentinian Fernando Novas found a skeleton of the meat eater Herrerasaurus in 1988 in Argentina. Earlier, in 1963, Victorino Herrera, a farmer, had found some bones of this same dinosaur. Sereno named the dinosaur in his honor.

1998
Professor Philip Currie (born 1949) made many discoveries in the badlands of Alberta, Canada. He also led expeditions to China, Mongolia, and South America. He helped to describe some of the first feathered dinosaurs, such as Caudipteurix in 1998.

Changing Ideas

New discoveries have often caused dinosaur experts to change their minds. For example, as scientists over the years found and studied more fossils of the dinosaur Iguanodon, they had to think again about what it looked like and how it moved. It is possible that new discoveries will make dinosaur experts change their minds again.

1825
Because of its teeth, dinosaur experts originally thought that Iguanodon looked like a huge iguana.

Late 1880s
By this time, experts decided it was some kind of fearsome dragon.

1900s
Some years later, experts saw it as a reptile, with its tail dragging along the ground.

Today
The latest discoveries have led experts to believe Iguanodon walked on all fours, with its tail held up off the ground.

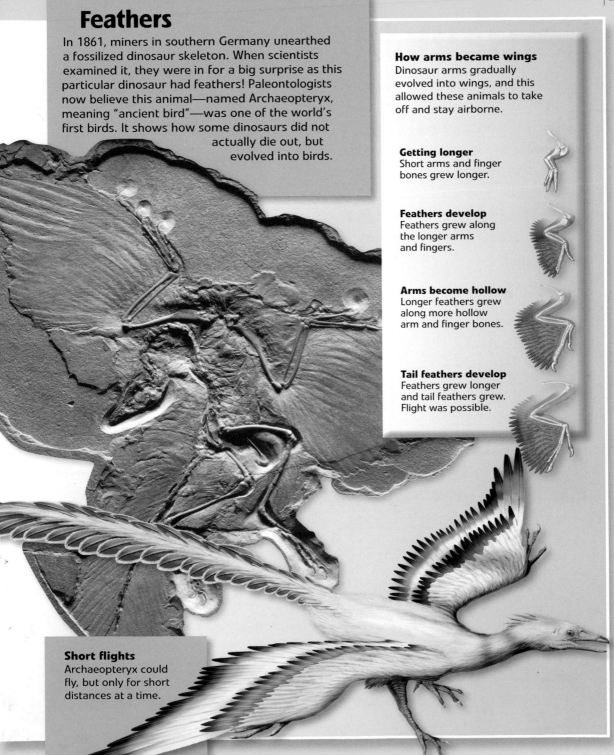

Feathers

In 1861, miners in southern Germany unearthed a fossilized dinosaur skeleton. When scientists examined it, they were in for a big surprise as this particular dinosaur had feathers! Paleontologists now believe this animal—named Archaeopteryx, meaning "ancient bird"—was one of the world's first birds. It shows how some dinosaurs did not actually die out, but evolved into birds.

How arms became wings
Dinosaur arms gradually evolved into wings, and this allowed these animals to take off and stay airborne.

Getting longer
Short arms and finger bones grew longer.

Feathers develop
Feathers grew along the longer arms and fingers.

Arms become hollow
Longer feathers grew along more hollow arm and finger bones.

Tail feathers develop
Feathers grew longer and tail feathers grew. Flight was possible.

Short flights
Archaeopteryx could fly, but only for short distances at a time.

Dinosaur Sites

Many dinosaur sites are areas where large numbers of dinosaurs have been discovered. Other sites are where the remains of individual dinosaurs or groups of dinosaurs have been found. Dinosaurs lived in these sites between 65 and 250 million years ago. When dinosaurs lived, these sites would have looked very different from how they look today.

3 Dinosaur Provincial Park, Alberta, Canada
The museum near this site displays many of the fine dinosaur fossils that were found here.

2 Hell Creek, Montana
Remains of some of the last dinosaurs to live on Earth have been found here.

1 Dinosaur National Monument, Utah
Remains of nearly 100 dinosaur species have been found here.

4 Solnhofen, Germany
The site where the first bird, Archaeopteryx, were discovered is also where the remains of the dinosaur Compsognathus was found.

5 Gobi Desert, Mongolia
The first-ever dinosaur nest was found in this region of shifting sands in 1922.

6 Liaoning, China
Many early birds and dinosaurs with feathers have been found at this site in northern China.

8 Ischigualasto Park, Argentina
Fossils of some of the earliest dinosaurs that ever lived were found here, near the base of the Andes mountains.

7 Dinosaur Cove, Australia
Dinosaur remains found here show that dinosaurs could live in cold places where there were long, dark winters.

Recent Finds

Some of the dinosaurs mentioned so far may sound familiar, but the dinosaur names on these pages probably do not because they were discovered only in the last few years. One day some of these dinosaurs will be very well known. Meanwhile, dinosaur hunters will continue to find new ones.

EOCARCHARIA

NAME MEANS: Dawn shark

LIVED: Early Cretaceous period

FOOD: Meat

SIZE: 23 feet (7 m) long

FOSSIL LOCATION: Niger

DATE FOUND: 2008

FUTALOGNKOSAURUS

NAME MEANS: Giant chief lizard

LIVED: Late Cretaceous period

FOOD: Plants

SIZE: 110 feet (33 m) long

FOSSIL LOCATION: Argentina

DATE FOUND: 2007

MEI LONG

NAME MEANS: Soundly sleeping dragon

LIVED: Early Cretaceous period

FOOD: Meat

SIZE: 110 feet (33 m) long

FOSSIL LOCATION: Argentina

DATE FOUND: 2007

EOCURSOR

NAME MEANS: Dawn runner

LIVED: Late Triassic period

FOOD: Plants

SIZE: 3 feet (1 m) long

FOSSIL LOCATIONS: South Africa; United States

DATE FOUND: 2007

UNAYSAURUS

NAME MEANS: Black water lizard

LIVED: Late Triassic period

FOOD: Plants

SIZE: 8 feet (2.5 m) long

FOSSIL LOCATION: Brazil

DATE FOUND: 2004

SCIPIONYX

NAME MEANS: Scipio's claw (after the geologist Scipione Breislak).

LIVED: Early Cretaceous period

FOOD: Meat

SIZE: 6 feet (2 m) long

FOSSIL LOCATION: Italy

DATE FOUND: 1998

GUANLONG

NAME MEANS: Crown dragon

LIVED: Late Jurassic period

FOOD: Meat

SIZE: 10 feet (3 m) long

FOSSIL LOCATION: China

DATE FOUND: 2006

ANTARCTOPELTA

NAME MEANS: Antarctic shield

LIVED: Late Cretaceous period

FOOD: Plants

SIZE: 13 feet (4 m) long

FOSSIL LOCATION: Antarctica

DATE FOUND: 2006

NOMINGIA

NAME MEANS: From Nomingiin (Gobi Desert)

LIVED: Late Cretaceous period

FOOD: Meat

SIZE: 5.5 feet (1.7 m) long

FOSSIL LOCATION: Mongolia

DATE FOUND: 2000

RUGOPS

NAME MEANS: Wrinkle face

LIVED: Late Cretaceous period

FOOD: Meat

SIZE: 23–26 feet (7–8 m) long

FOSSIL LOCATION: Niger

DATE FOUND: 2004

Fact File

How big or small could dinosaurs be? How clever or how dumb were they? How many of them hunted other animals for their food? Here are the answers to these and other fascinating questions about these prehistoric creatures.

WHAT DINOSAURS ATE

Many dinosaurs were fierce hunters. But more than two thirds of all the dinosaurs that ever lived ate only plants. The largest plant eaters were slow movers, while meat eaters were often very fast movers.

Plant eaters   Meat eaters

How heavy?

An African elephant can weigh 6.5 tons (6 t). Here's how different dinosaurs compared.

Protoceratops
An African elephant was 11 times heavier than this dinosaur.

Tyrannosaurus rex
This dinosaur was as big and heavy as an elephant.

Argentinosaurus
This huge dinosaur weighed as much as 17 elephants.

How big?

How do humans and other animals, such as a giraffe, compare in size with the largest and smallest dinosaurs?

Microraptor
The tiniest dinosaur was 30 inches (76 cm) long and 10.5 inches (27 cm) tall.

Giraffe
18 feet
(5.5 m) tall

Boy
4.5 feet
(1.4 m) tall

Gigantosaurus
The largest meat eater was 47 feet (14 m) long and 12 feet (3.6 m) tall.

Seismosaurus
The longest dinosaur was 150 feet (45 m) long and 18 feet (5.5 m) tall.

Long or short claws?
Compare these meat-eating dinosaurs' claws with the claws of a modern harpy eagle.

Harpy eagle
This bird's claws are 5 inches (13 cm) long.

Deinonychus
This dinosaur had sharp back claws that were 4 inches (10 cm) long.

Therizinosaurus
This dinosaur had front claws that were 36 inches (91 cm) long.

Smart or not smart?
Dinosaurs were not as smart as today's birds and mammals.

Humans
Humans are the smartest animals on Earth.

Velociraptor
This hunter was one of the smartest of all dinosaurs.

Stegosaurus
This plant eater was not very bright at all.

How much brain power?
As a general rule, comparing the size of an animal's brain to the size of its whole body is an indication of its intelligence. This means animals with large brains in small bodies are the most intelligent.

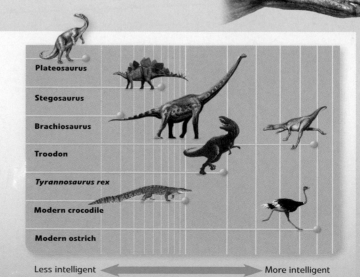

Plateosaurus
Stegosaurus
Brachiosaurus
Troodon
Tyrannosaurus rex
Modern crocodile
Modern ostrich

Less intelligent ⟵⟶ More intelligent

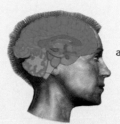

Mix and Match

Can you find the word on the left of the page that describes each picture?

1 skeleton

2 paleontologist

3 mammoth

4 trackways

5 Maiasaura

6 Gobi Desert

Glossary

Argentina (ar-jen-TEE-nuh) A vast country that occupies most of the southern and southwestern part of South America.

badlands (BAD-landz) Very dry, sandy, and rocky regions where very few plants or grasses can grow.

Cretaceous period (krih-TAY-shus PIR-ee-ud) The period between 144 and 65 million years ago. It was the last period in which dinosaurs existed.

crust (KRUST) The solid, outer part of Earth on which we live. This top layer of our planet is about 25 miles (40 km) deep. The bottom of the oceans is also part of Earth's crust.

dinosaurs (DY-nuh-sorz) A group of reptiles that were the dominant animals on Earth for about 160 million years, until about 65 million years ago, when most died out.

fossil (FO-sul) A part of a plant or animal that has turned to stone or that has left a print of its shape in rock.

ice age (YS AYJ) A period of time when the whole world remained very cold and when a large part of Earth's surface was covered with ice.

iguana (ih-GWAH-nuh) A large lizard that has spines along its back and a flap of skin under its chin and neck. Iguanas live in tropical North America and South America.

Jurassic period (ju-RA-sik PIR-ee-ud) The period between 208 and 144 million years ago. Many new kinds of dinosaurs appeared during the Jurassic period.

mammal (MA-mul) A warm-blooded animal that has a backbone and hair on its body. Adult female mammals feed their young with milk from their own body. Humans are mammals.

mammoth (MA-muth) An elephant-like animal with long hair that lived in northern parts of the world until about 10,000 years ago.

Mongolia (mawn-GOH-lee-uh) A country in northern Asia, between China and Russia.

paleontologist (pay-lee-on-TO-luh-jist) A scientist who studies fossils to learn about animals and plants in ancient times.

reptile (REP-tyl) A cold-blooded animal that has a backbone, breathes air, and has scaly skin. Dinosaurs were reptiles. Lizards, crocodiles, alligators, turtles, and snakes are all present-day reptiles.

sauropod (SOR-uh-pod) One of a group of four-legged, plant-eating dinosaurs that had a very long neck and tail. Sauropods were some of the largest animals ever to walk upon Earth.

skeleton (SKEH-leh-tun) The way all the bones in an animal's body are arranged. The skeleton gives the body strength and shape.

technician (tek-NIH-shen) A person who prepares materials for a special purpose. Technicians can prepare dinosaur bones and fossils before they are assembled and displayed in museums.

trackways (TRAK-wayz) Footprints of dinosaurs and other ancient animals.

Triassic period (try-A-sik PIR-ee-ud)) The period between 245 and 208 million years ago. The first dinosaurs appeared in the middle of this period, about 228 million years ago.

Index

Websites

Due to the changing nature of Internet links, PowerKids Press has developed an online list of websites related to the subject of this book. This site is updated regularly. Please use this link to access the list: www.powerkidslinks.com/disc/dino/